I LOVE MY WORK

I LOVE MY WORK

SIX STUDIES TO HELP CHURCHES
UNDERSTAND AND EQUIP
CHRISTIANS IN THE WORKPLACE

Robin Scurlock

and

Steve Goss

Terra Nova Publications

Published in Great Britain by
Terra Nova Publications Ltd
PO Box 2400, Bradford on Avon, Wiltshire BA15 2YN

ISBN 1901949184

Printed in Great Britain by Cox & Wyman, Reading

Contents

ACKNOWLEDGEMENTS

We would like to acknowledge with grateful thanks the significant contribution of Bruce Jenkins.

We would also like to thank many others who offered advice, prayer and encouragement through various drafts, including: James Allcock OBE, Michael Benford, Alistair Burt MP, Tony Collins, Andrew Cornes, Lynn Green, Mark Greene, Sarah Hurrell, Don Latham, Andy Macnamara, Malcolm Matson, David Prior, Andrew Raynes, Hisham Saba, Jeff Taylor, Paul Valler, John Williams and the many and various ministers around the UK on whom we piloted early versions of *I Love My Work*.

Finally, we would like to thank our wives, Fay and Zoë, and our families, for putting up with the inevitable growing pains which accompanied the production of this book.

WHAT'S THE PROBLEM?

A recent 'Marketplace Meditation'[1] by Os Hillman amusingly illustrates the truth that the task of gaining a biblical perspective on the world of work has been badly neglected.

> 'If Satan and his demons had a board meeting and your name came before the board, what would they say? Would they say that you are one of their most feared enemies and they needed to keep many demons harassing and opposing you? Or would they say, "Gentlemen, this person poses no threat to our activities. Leave him alone. He needs no help from us."?'

Undoubtedly, it is the case that many working Christians are ill-equipped to respond to the pressures around them, and their churches have struggled to keep pace.

London Bible College (LBC) and the London Institute for Contemporary Christianity (LICC), founded by John Stott in 1982, are two organisations working to address this and other perceived teaching gaps. Surveys conducted by Mark Greene, Director of the LICC, provide some alarming statistics:

- 50% of Christians have never heard a single sermon on work.

- Over 70% have never been taught a theology of work.

---

[1] See www.crosswalk.com and www.marketplaceleaders.org

● Fewer than 25% have ever been asked by their minister about their witness at work.

The problem might well be seen to originate within a church that has become a little unbalanced in its understanding of issues such as 'work' and 'calling'.

This book is a resource to help the church regain some of this lost balance. It provides some basic materials to help congregations and small groups begin to rediscover why Christians really can *love* their work —and perhaps it can help to change those statistics!

CALLING ALL CHURCH LEADERS!

It was he who gave some to be apostles, some to be prophets, some to be evangelists, and some to be pastors and teachers, to prepare God's people for works of service, so that the body of Christ may be built up...

Ephesians 4:11–12

One of the purposes of any local church is to 'prepare God's people for works of service'. But where will those works of service take place?

Many of us in leadership roles in local churches might instinctively respond, 'in the church'. That is a good answer, and it is certainly right. But it is far from the whole picture.

Where does your congregation spend most of its time? In today's world, most people spend up to 70% of their waking hours at work, be that paid work or unpaid work in the home or the community.

Do you believe that they cannot exercise their God-given ministry where they spend most of their time? Of course, you don't! But we have unwittingly managed to give them that impression.

It might be interesting to ask yourself a couple of questions: when was the last time a sermon on work was preached in your church? Or when was the last time you prayed for someone's secular work in your church? There is at least a grain of truth in the observation that, in order to be prayed for in most of our churches, you have either to be in 'full-time' Christian work ... or sick!

As church leaders, we quite rightly have a very strong sense of God's calling. This can lead us to *act* as if the only important ministry is the one exercised directly in the church. The focus therefore tends to be on our own internal needs and on how to run a successful and growing membership organisation.

The role of the apostles, prophets, evangelists, pastors and teachers mentioned in Ephesians 4 is to prepare our people for the works of service that God has called *them* to. We can all too easily suck them into the works of service that he has called *us* to do!

There are some important questions that we need to consider:

- What God-given ministry have these people been given?

- How can the church help them to exercise these ministries where they work?

THE PROBLEM

As many have observed, the church has largely adopted a secular view of work. The result is that few Christians nowadays see their jobs as spiritual service. Few know that what they spend most of their time doing is actually what God wants them to be doing. And that leads to confusion and a lack of spiritual authenticity. It works like this:

- We feel that our work is not really important in the eyes of other Christians (or perhaps God himself).

- We do not find much help in the church for the moral dilemmas we face daily in our jobs.

- We still find our jobs enjoyable and stimulating.

- We end up dividing our lives into sacred and secular compartments that are rarely allowed to mix.

It is helpful to realise that this is a comparatively recent development. The Reformers, for example, taught clearly that every Christian had a calling or 'vocation' —a butcher was equally as called as a missionary and each was to approach their work as service to God. Tyndale said:

'There is difference betwixt washing of dishes and preaching of the word of God; but as touching to please God, none at all.'

DOES IT MATTER?

It matters because Christians who work in secular employment can feel terribly isolated.

They do not see that what they spend most of their time doing is a gift from God or a great opportunity to use their God-given talents. Work instead becomes a necessary evil, a kind of punishment, something to be tolerated or suffered in anticipation of the really important things of life — either working in the church or bankrolling it financially.

While these aspects are important, to see our work as valuable only in these contexts blunts our spiritual effectiveness and leaves many people confused and spiritually impotent. God calls some to missionary organisations, some to the public sector, some into business and some to the home. All are in full-time Christian service.

Is it right to pray for someone working as an accountant at, for example, Tearfund or Oxfam? Yes, of course!

Is it right to pray for an accountant in a large multinational corporation who gives regularly and generously to Tearfund or Oxfam? Yes, of course!

Paul says, '*whatever* you do, do it all for the glory of God' (I Corinthians 10:31). God is interested in all aspects of what he has called his people to do. But the church often appears not to be!

THE OPPORTUNITY FOR THE CHURCH

The impact of the church genuinely preparing its membership for acts of service in the secular workplace could be huge. We see in Ephesians 4 that the whole point of preparing God's people for works of service is 'so that the body of Christ may be built up'.

Recently, we spent considerable effort along with a team of others from local churches conducting a PR campaign for an evangelistic initiative — trying in one way to 'build up' the body of Christ as instructed. The campaign went very well — we leafleted tens of thousands of homes and got coverage in the local media. As a result, we attracted around 20–30 people to join introductory courses on faith and Christianity.

Yet might there not be an even better way?

Where do most Christians come into most contact with people who are struggling to make sense of a changing world, who are puzzled, confused, uncertain, hurting, or who have deep spiritual needs? —At work! Where is the difference that God makes in our lives most obvious... While knocking on doors in the neighbourhood...? Or while spending 40, 50 or 60 hours a week under pressure in the office, school, hospital, shop or factory?

Most of our people spend most of their day rubbing shoulders with colleagues who have no Christian faith. Imagine what would happen if they really got hold of the fact that they are children of the living God specifically called by him to be in that place with those people!

Yet in our churches sit many who, instead of touching people's lives with the gospel, are struggling to make sense of some fundamental questions on which the church has for too long seemed completely silent:

- How can I best serve God in my job?

- Is it right for a Christian not to do 'full-time' Christian service?

- Is it OK to earn lots of money?

- How should I set priorities when job, family and church make conflicting demands?

Instead of leaving them there with their vague sense of unease, we leaders need to release them into the world fully prepared for what they will find there, with a strong sense of calling and support.

We need to tell them that:

- The church is supposed to function as a body with different people called to do different things.

- The important thing is to identify what God wants you to do and then do it.

- If this means going off on missionary journeys, then so be it. If it means remaining in your job and serving through your practical skills, then so be it. If it means running a business and thereby being able to help support the fellowship financially, then so be it.

We need to reassure them that:

- As with many converts to Christianity in the New Testament, there is no reason to suppose that they had to leave their everyday jobs or to consider them any less important as a result of their conversion.

If we can help others to look upon their jobs as God's calling, we will find that they will shine out with his love and power instead of being weighed down by doubt and uncertainty. And that will make a difference to those they meet day by day.

It is our prayer that you will find these resources useful for the purpose of preparing the people that God has entrusted to your care for the works of service that he has called them to do.

Robin Scurlock & Steve Goss

SUGGESTIONS FOR USE

Each chapter is presented in two parts:

- **Presentation Themes** — for use in a service/workshop, as a talk or as a discussion framework.

- **Questions for Study** — particularly good for small group follow-up.

There are several ways in which you might use it in a local church.

1. A special series of services or workshops
You might consider introducing the theme of work with a special service —Harvest might be a particularly appropriate time when we thank God for the fruits of our work.

2. Small group studies
The chapters lend themselves very well to a stand-alone series, either as part of a cell or small group programme or as a special series of meetings for people in their workplaces.

3. Private study
The book is a valuable resource for private study for those who want to understand their own calling.

4. Training of ministers and church leaders
The book also provides a good introduction for leaders to some of the work issues faced by their church membership.

Chapter One

GOD'S VIEW OF WORK

The LORD God took the man and put him in the Garden of Eden to work it and take care of it.

Genesis 2:15

INTRODUCTION

Christians in secular employment, or who are considering entering it, can often be faced with numerous work-related questions. After all, a person's job demands a lot of their time, and prime time too.

- Is working in a secular job the best use of my time and talents?

- What type of job will offer the most fulfilling career path?

- Is it right to devote my time and efforts to making commercial profit?

- How should my attitude to work differ from that of my non-Christian colleagues?

There are many pressures to accept what the world presents as normal practice and behaviour, which can result in a real temptation, for example, to compromise our personal beliefs and standards of behaviour. At the same time, there is the genuine danger of giving our work too high a priority, and to make our careers all-important.

The difficulties of thinking through some of these issues, particularly in Western society, has led to what is commonly known as a 'sacred/secular' divide, where secular occupations are viewed as second-rate to what the church calls 'full-time' sacred ministry. This often results in a vague feeling of unease amongst those of us in non-church roles, that perhaps we have not been really open to what God wants us to be doing.

This chapter confirms that such a division in the world of work is not what God intended. In his eyes there is no division between what we call 'secular' and 'sacred'.

PRESENTATION THEMES

- God created work as part of his design for the world.

- There is dignity in a wide variety of work.

- Work, like everything else, is affected by the curse that came after the Fall.

- Even after the Fall, work remains a God-given blessing.

- Our task is to work with God in the way he originally intended.

- We are to work for the majority of our time.

- God will use our work to shape our character in Christ.

> ## God created work as part of his design for the world.

The Bible portrays God when we first meet him as doing the *work* of creation. God himself is a worker. An important part of God's work was the creation of human beings who were made in his very image. It is not surprising, therefore, to discover that we have an urge to work just as our Father does.

> The LORD God took the man and put him in the Garden of Eden to work it and take care of it.
>
> *Genesis 2:15*

When the world was perfect, and human beings had not yet sinned, Eden was not a playground, but a place of work. Work was what God gave us to do as our intended occupation. Work is therefore not a punishment or a human contrivance but a blessing.

> And the LORD God commanded the man, "You are free to eat from any tree in the garden."
>
> *Genesis 2:16*

Adam cultivated the ground and then ate the produce from it. The provision of our basic needs is normally directly dependent upon work. The connection between work and enjoying the fruits of our efforts is reinforced in other places in the Bible:

> For the Scripture says, "Do not muzzle the ox while it is treading out the grain," and "The worker deserves his wages."
>
> *I Timothy 5:18*

The reverse is also true. The idle person who will not work must not eat.

For even when we were with you, we gave you this rule: "If a man will not work, he shall not eat."

II Thessalonians 3:10

There is dignity in a wide variety of work.

There are many different types of work to which we can devote our attention —investigating this world, gaining an understanding of it, discovering its potential, harnessing its resources, and using them in a useful way.

God blessed them and said to them, "Be fruitful and increase in number; fill the earth and subdue it. Rule over the fish of the sea and the birds of the air and over every living creature that moves on the ground."

Genesis 1:28

We take for granted many aspects of our world which originally had to be discovered by a process of subduing the earth:

- Soil can be cultivated, crops planted and techniques for cooking developed.

- Trees can be grown, felled, machined and used for shelter, furniture and paper.

- Metals may be mined, their properties studied, and then used in many applications.

> **Work, like everything else, is affected by the curse that came after the Fall.**

Work is not all joy, satisfaction and productivity. Before sin entered the world at the Fall, the fruits gained from work were commensurate to the effort. Now the effort can often far exceed the gain.

To Adam he said, "Because you listened to your wife and ate from the tree about which I commanded you, 'You must not eat of it,' "Cursed is the ground because of you; through painful toil you will eat of it all the days of your life. It will produce thorns and thistles for you, and you will eat the plants of the field. By the sweat of your brow you will eat your food until you return to the ground, since from it you were taken; for dust you are and to dust you will return."

Genesis 3:17–19

Work is now accompanied by sorrow, hardship and frustration.

What does a man get for all the toil and anxious striving with which he labours under the sun? All his days his work is pain and grief: even at night his mind does not rest. This too is meaningless.

Ecclesiastes 2:22–23

> **Even after the Fall, work
> remains a God-given blessing.**

God's plan for humankind included work even after the Fall. The Fall only partially destroyed its nature and purpose.

> So the LORD God banished him from the Garden of Eden to work the ground from which he had been taken.
>
> *Genesis 3:23*

It is clear that work changed, but that does not mean that work itself is intrinsically bad (even though it may seem that way at 7 o'clock on a Monday morning!)

The intention was for humankind to continue to work. Work itself is not a curse or even a necessary evil. Indeed, Jesus himself spent most of his life at work as a carpenter in a small business.

Most of us can get excited about our work. That is because we can feel God's original purpose within us. This is particularly true when we do something creative, or when we do something of value for someone else. The Fall can never obscure the fantastic benefits of one of God's greatest gifts. It can still give us a sense of achievement and fulfilment.

> **Our task is to work with God in
> the way he originally intended.**

In our work we will want to make every effort to get back as close as we can to the original blueprint. Whenever what we do reflects what God originally intended, we can be certain that God is pleased.

That original plan is reflected in the work God himself does. Looking at some of its attributes can help us.

It is creative

God is constantly working. Although he never changes, he is constantly finding new ways of expressing his love and his goodness. He is never satisfied with simply repeating past successes.

"Behold I am doing a new thing."

Isaiah 43:19

Similarly, work that will be a blessing to us and not a curse should be stimulating. God did not perform the work needed to create the universe and to create human beings because he was bored or lonely. He did it because he is supremely creative.

It is primarily for others

There is nothing selfish in what God does. The Creation reflects God's glory but he created it for our benefit. The life of Jesus illustrates the way God tirelessly works for others. Jesus never put himself first, but always cared for other people. Working for our own ends is not enough. We will find that if our work is primarily for our own good and does not give us opportunities to serve others, then it is not fulfilling.

It is in partnership with humankind

God made a conscious decision to work in partnership with human beings. It is clear that he is all-powerful, that he can do anything he wants, yet he makes a deliberate choice to work with us.

In his book *Issues Facing Christians Today*, John Stott defines work that pleases God as, 'the expenditure of energy (manual or mental or both) in the service of others, which brings fulfilment to the worker, benefit to the community, and glory to God.' He reminds us of the old story of a gardener, who shows a parson a beautiful garden, with its herbaceous borders at their summer best. The clergyman is so impressed that he starts to praise God. Unhappy that God should get the praise when he himself had put in so much work, the gardener points out that the clergyman should have seen the garden when God had it all to himself!

The gardener, of course, was wrong about the matter of praise (all the glory goes to God for *all* good things, including those good things that flow from the work of our hands, and the gardener's talent and abilities came from God).

The truth is that God has both provided the raw materials and graciously chosen to use humankind to bring him glory and to fulfil his purposes for the world. All work should be viewed in the light of this ultimate partnership.

We are to work for the majority of our time.

Six days you shall labour and do all your work, but the seventh day is a Sabbath to the LORD your God. On it you shall not do any work, neither you, nor your son or daughter, nor your manservant or maidservant, nor your animals, nor the alien within your gates.

Exodus 20:9–10

The fourth commandment requires us to work for the majority of our time (six days out of seven). It also demands one day of rest in the seven for us all, including anyone employed by us. It is therefore right that work should occupy much of our time, however we choose to define it.

We may no longer *need* to work all of the remaining six days in order to support ourselves but we must avoid idleness.

In the name of the Lord Jesus Christ, we command you, brothers, to keep away from every brother who is idle and does not live according to the teaching you received from us.

II Thessalonians 3:6

> **God will use our work to shape our character in Christ.**

What if your work does not seem to reflect much of God's original intention and seems like, well, hard work? Should you simply change jobs?

Although there might be a case for that in certain circumstances, the reality is that our work this side of eternity will never fully reflect work as God intended. In fact, far from wanting us to look for a change when circumstances are tough, God will often want to use those difficult circumstances to speak to us.

Perhaps he will want to help us understand that, although our work is meant to be fulfilling and satisfying, it was never meant to define who we are. It is all too easy for us to try and get our sense of well-being and self-worth only from our work. Christians should have a completely different basis for self-worth:

> How great is the love the Father has lavished on us that we should be called children of God! And that is what we are!
>
> *I John 3:1*

What better basis could there be for self-worth than knowing that truth?

Whether we find our work rewarding or relentless, whether we are a high powered, well-paid executive or have a humbler role, knowing that we are children of God is the starting place.

Conclusion

We are all made to work, and we will always want to work because we are made in God's image. Work continues to be a good thing in spite of the Fall, and we will still be working in eternity when Christ returns. The drudgery the Fall has added will be removed for ever.

No longer will there be any curse. The throne of God and of the Lamb will be in the city, and his servants will serve him.

Revelation 22:3

While we are waiting for this, we will want our work to reflect God's original intentions as far as is possible, using the work that our Heavenly Father himself does as our model.

QUESTIONS FOR STUDY

1. Work is a gift from God. Do you agree?

2. What effect did the Fall have on work?

3. What effects of the Fall do you see in your day-to-day working life?

4. Why do you think work is so important to most people? How does this importance vary according to the age of the people concerned?

5. Where should Christians get their sense of self-worth —from work or from something else?

6. Why do you think that God wants to be our work 'partner' even though he could do a much better job on his own?

7. What do you think this suggests about how he values his creation? What can we learn from this, which applies to what we do the next time we go to work?

8. Assuming we accept that God is interested, what effect should that have upon our attitude to work?

Chapter Two

ARE YOU IN THE RIGHT PLACE?

Whatever you do, work at it with all your heart, as working for the Lord not for men, since you know that you will receive an inheritance from the Lord as a reward. It is the Lord Christ you are serving.

Colossians 3:23

INTRODUCTION

For most Christians, work takes up our very best waking hours and uses up more of our resources than any other part of our life. It is important to know that it is a major part of our God-given calling, that we are not squandering our energies on something that is not pleasing to our Father.

Some Christians consider that 'full-time' Christian work—in other words, working for a missionary-based organisation—is the only legitimate occupation, or at least that other forms of work are less important. The church, probably unwittingly, reinforces this by concentrating its prayer support and encouragement on those in 'full-time' Christian work, to the neglect of those in other occupations.

This view, while understandable, is unbiblical and may contribute to the guilt and paralysis that many Christians in secular occupations feel.

The truth is that God calls different people to different roles. All are 'full-time' callings. The key issue is to know that where you are now is where God wants you to be.

PRESENTATION THEMES

- God wants us to know him and to reflect the character of Jesus Christ.

- God has a unique calling for us that covers every area of our lives.

- Our particular position in God's kingdom has never been occupied before.

- God sometimes calls us to new things and his timing is always perfect.

- Where we spend most of our time is where God is most likely to develop our character.

- So ... are you in the right place?

> **God wants us to know him, and to
> reflect the character of Jesus Christ.**

We tend to spend a lot of time and energy agonising about whether we are *doing* the right thing — whether we should pursue a particular career or line of business, for example. That is what this chapter is about. But we need to recognise that God is primarily not so much interested in what we *do* but in who we *are* and what we are *like*.

Do you know what God's main goals for your life are? Actually they have very little to do with what you *do*.

KNOWING GOD

> But whatever was to my profit I now consider loss for the sake of Christ. What is more, I consider everything a loss compared to the surpassing greatness of knowing Christ Jesus my Lord, for whose sake I have lost all things. I consider them rubbish, that I may gain Christ and be found in him, not having a righteousness of my own that comes from the law, but that which is through faith in Christ—the righteousness that comes from God and is by faith. I want to know Christ and the power of his resurrection and the fellowship of sharing in his sufferings....
>
> *Philippians 3:7–10*

God wants us to know him in a real, very personal way. Paul had every reason to feel good about himself when looking at his external achievements and his position in society. But he came to see that none of these achievements meant anything at all if he did not know Jesus Christ. In fact he considered them all 'rubbish' (a strong word in the original Greek that could also be translated 'dung').

The commands of God guide us to what really is the best for us. Such obedience to him is the fruit of real knowledge and love for him, and this flows from his self-revelation to us in Jesus Christ. Love, faith and trust in God are intimately linked.

Everything flows from whether or not we really know God in a daily relationship.

BECOMING 'CHRIST LIKE' IN CHARACTER

> We also rejoice in our sufferings, because we know that suffering produces perseverance; perseverance, character; and character, hope. And hope does not disappoint us, because God has poured out his love into our hearts by the Holy Spirit, whom he has given us.
>
> *Romans 5:3–5*

He wants to turn us into people who reflect his character. Whereas we tend to focus on ministry and tangible results — 'what should I do?' — God focuses on character: 'what am I like?' So, in one sense, God does not mind whether you are an engineer, a missionary or a secretary, but rather what *kind* of engineer, missionary or secretary you are.

The key, here, is set out for us by Paul. He teaches Christians that (we) 'reflect the Lord's glory' and, '...are being transformed into his likeness....' This change in men and women can only be brought about by the Lord. (See II Corinthians 3:16–18).

> **God has a unique calling for us
> that covers every area of our lives.**

Having settled that the main issue is our character and what we are *like*, then, of course, there are things that God calls us to *do*. The idea of 'calling', or vocation, is foundational to a work life that pleases God.

'Calling' can be described as the confident expression of knowing that God has created a unique space for the person you are, and that by filling that space, you cannot be in a better place.

All Christians have a general calling, irrespective of who they are and where they practise their faith.

Therefore go and make disciples of all nations, baptising them in the name of the Father and of the Son and of the Holy Spirit.

Matthew 28:19

You are the salt of the earth.... You are the light of the world.... let your light shine before men, that they may see your good deeds and praise your Father in heaven.

Matthew 5:13–16

But each one of us also has a specific calling.

For we are God's workmanship, created in Christ Jesus to do good works, which God prepared in advance for us to do.

Ephesians 2:10

It is exciting to realise that there are some unique things that God prepared for you to do before you even knew him.

> **Our particular position in God's kingdom
> has never been occupied before.**

We all find ourselves in a certain place which is unique in the history of God's kingdom. This will combine important influences in our lives —our upbringing, education, ambitions, natural gifts (for example musical or sporting abilities), occupation, whether we are single or married.

Only I can be the husband to my wife, the father to my children and the son of my parents. Only I can be the neighbour to those next door to me, the person sitting at the desk next to my colleague, the person occupying my place in the local church.

> It was he who gave some to be apostles, some to be prophets, some to be evangelists, and some to be pastors and teachers.
>
> *Ephesians 4:11*

> Paul, a servant of Christ Jesus, called to be an apostle and set apart for the gospel of God.
>
> *Romans 1:1*

The things that God has prepared in advance for us to do will be different to what others are called to do — not better or worse; just different.

God's call on our lives does not differentiate between 'church' and 'secular' activities. The Bible makes no such distinction. All activities are of equal importance to God provided they are exercised according to God's will. There is no question of your calling being any less worthy than anyone else's, including those in 'full-time' Christian work. If your calling is to be an accountant, a Boeing pilot or a street sweeper, it is every bit as worthwhile as 'full-time' Christian ministry. It's the place God wants you to be —and what could be more exciting than knowing that's where you are!

CALLED OR DRIVEN?[1]

It is all too easy for us simply to let circumstances drive us and never actually spend time seriously asking God what he is calling us to do. Are you a called person or a driven person?

- Called People understand stewardship, of time, talents and money.
- Called People know exactly who they are.
- Called People possess an unwavering sense of purpose.
- Called People understand unswerving commitment.
- Called People enjoy peace, satisfaction and contentment.

Gordon MacDonald wrote, 'Change can begin when such a person faces up that he/she is operating according to drives and not calls. That discovery is usually made in the blinding, searching light of an encounter with Christ. The person seeking relief from drivenness will find it wise to listen to mentors and critics who speak Christ's words to us today — after all this is one purpose of church fellowship.'

[1] See *Ordering your Private World*, Highland Books. Used by permission

God sometimes calls us to new things and his timing is always perfect.

Becoming a Christian is such a significant moment in our lives that it can cause us to re-assess our priorities, including our jobs. We may certainly need to test our behaviour against a new set of standards, but change for its own sake is not necessarily the right thing.

Each one should remain in the situation which he was in when God called him. Were you a slave when you were called? Don't let it trouble you —although if you can gain your freedom, do so.

I Corinthians 7:20–21

Paul counsels the married to remain married (even when their marriage partners are unconverted), and tells the newly converted slave to remain contentedly in his position unless an opportunity arises to change.

We are not to consider our situation when we are converted as being unworthy (unless, of course, it is inherently sinful) but as the place God has called us to be until he tells us otherwise.

Of course our lives are not cast in concrete when we are converted. We need to be constantly aware that God will have new things for us to do. Sometimes this may involve a complete change. God can and does move people on over time so that we can develop as Christians, and learn to trust him more. We should never be afraid of change, and should be open to him in prayer. If we are single we may marry, and if a better employment opportunity comes our way, we may take it — if the Lord directs.

When God called Jesus to leave his carpentry business and embark upon an entirely new direction for his life, he obeyed. For us too, obedience is the most important thing.

While they were worshipping the Lord and fasting, the Holy Spirit said, "Set apart for me Barnabas and Saul for the work to which I have called them."

Acts 13:2

Barnabas and Paul were acting as effective leaders in the church. Yet God called them away. It may not have made much sense to them, but they chose to obey. Being where God wants us, doing what God wants us to do, is where we will find blessing.

God never makes it difficult for us to hear what he is saying —but he will only speak if we are serious about hearing his voice. The call to Barnabas and Paul was determined by prayer and fasting.

> **Where we spend most of our time is where God is most likely to develop our character.**

Most people spend between 50% and 70% of their waking lives engaged in some form of work. The definition of work will vary depending on circumstance, as will whether it is paid or unpaid. However, a significant proportion of our energies are devoted to activities which we call work.

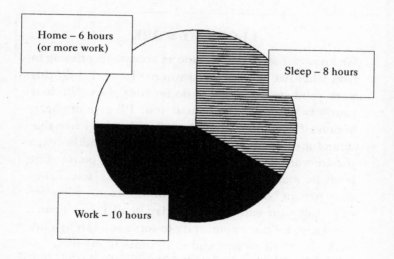

God uses these day-to-day circumstances to build our character — sometimes in adversity of some kind. So what do you do if your job seems hopeless? Change jobs? No — hang on in there and grow! There may be legitimate reasons to

change job, but not if you're just running away from difficulties. You will just have to learn somewhere else. God won't
move you on until you have.

We need to learn to 'bloom where we are planted'. In
other words, learn to embrace difficulties as opportunities to
grow more Christ-like. When we understand their real
purpose, we will genuinely rejoice like Paul when we
experience suffering and hurt.

We are required to be 'salt' and 'light' where he has
placed us. We are all full-time workers for Christ regardless
of our physical location or who pays our wages. Perhaps this
means having the faith to start a prayer meeting in the office,
neighbourhood or factory.

I LOVE MY WORK

We know our work can become an acceptable offering to
God when we are prepared to say, 'Lord, I'll do this
work you have given me to do for your glory. I'll do it
your way to please and honour you. I'll give my best,
because I want you to be pleased with this. I live this
area of my life for you because I love you and because
you are worthy of my obedience, service and praise. Let
Jesus be manifest in all I do in my workplace. Bring
glory to your Name through my work, because I live for
you. Let your will be done today in all I do. Thank
you, Lord, for this opportunity to serve you through my
work. Be glorified now and at all times in my life'.

(Prayer extract from *Champions for God at Work*, David
Kellett, published by Terra Nova Publications, p.49.)

So... are you in the right place?

Remain in me, and I will remain in you. No branch can bear fruit by itself; it must remain in the vine. Neither can you bear fruit unless you remain in me.

John 15:4

'Am I in the right place?' can be answered very easily. It is not so much to do with where you actually work. If you are 'remaining' in Christ, you are in the right place and you can expect fruit to come. If you are taking matters into your own hands and focusing too much on 'doing' then you need to come back to the vine and learn to 'remain' in him again.

But having got this fundamental part of our orientation right, then it is important that we see our daily work activity as part of our unique calling from the Lord.

Everyone can and should know what the Lord is calling them to do.

If we have a problem with knowing what God wants, it is usually more to do with our reluctance to listen and respond rather than God's refusal to make his will clear. It can be a question of timing —nearly, but not yet.

Being genuinely open can involve considerable agonising and heart searching. Our feelings can be deceptive. We need to be sure that any calling we feel is not simply our wish for security, or driven by selfish motives. Prayerful support from mature Christian friends can be helpful in discerning the will of God. Mature Christians recognise that the very best place to be is where God wants them —no matter how strange or difficult it may at first appear.

Maybe this is the time to come before God and ask him openly and honestly about whether or not you are where he wants you to be —to wrestle with the subtle temptations that make you afraid to stay put or to change.

Conclusion

Given that many people spend more than half their lives 'working', it is important to know that we are in the right place:

- We will work in God's strength and anointing.
- We will have the resilience to work through difficult times.
- We will have faith to know God's blessing 'in all things'.
- We will not put our trust in things that do not last (job title, promotions, status).

Christians in 'secular' jobs have the same opportunity to put God first in their work and to bear fruit as Christians in 'full-time' service. Our jobs are part of a high and holy calling from God himself!

QUESTIONS FOR STUDY

1.   Do you agree that knowing Jesus and developing our character are God's most important priorities for our lives? (Use the Bible to back your answer up).

2.   What do we mean by 'calling'? Give an example from your own life of when you were called to do something. What is the opposite of being called?

3.   To what can we be called? Marriage? A particular job? A holiday destination? What level of detail and guidance should we expect from God?

4.   Should we expect to have a specific work calling?

   • to a profession

   • to a company or organisation

   • to a career

5.   Calvin used the idea of vocation to encourage loyalty to a particular area of work. Writing on I Corinthians 7, he says:

   'Each should be content with his calling and persist in it, and not be eager to change to something else … (Paul) condemns the restlessness which prevents individuals from remaining contentedly as they are.'

   How should we understand Calvin's teaching in the light of today's job mobility and career expectations?

6.   What sort of work carries the most importance to God? For example, paid or unpaid? Voluntary or salaried? Commercial or public sector?

7. How can you find out what God has called you to do? Do you think God has a plan for your life, and if so, how has this been revealed to date?

8. Do you tend to be a 'called' or a 'driven' person?

To Work or Not to Work

- God is calling me to be a missionary in Peru.

- I'm applying for a job in another company.

- I'm taking early retirement to give more time to the Lord.

- It's hard to get to the prayer meeting because of my working hours.

- It's not necessarily a better job, but the money is significantly better.

What do these statements tell us about our understanding of calling at work?

[From 'Wake up to Work' © Geoff Shattock, published by Scripture Union, 1999 and used with permission.]

Chapter Three

SUCCESS AND FAILURE

But whatever was to my profit I now consider loss for the sake of Christ. What is more, I consider everything a loss compared to the surpassing greatness of knowing Christ Jesus my Lord, for whose sake I have lost all things.

Philippians 3:7–8

INTRODUCTION

In our society, material success has become an increasingly important life goal. And in Western culture, many people derive their identity from this success.

In his book *The Success Factor*, Denis Haack attributes this need to the fact that Western culture has embraced relativism. This is a belief system which assumes that: there is no absolute truth; there is no right or wrong; no religion has a monopoly on truth but that there is some truth in all of them; and, provided you are not hurting anyone else, anything goes.

For people with no other belief system, the only way of making life meaningful is to be 'successful' in the eyes of their peers.

Christians have to choose which type of 'success' to aim for. If we do not derive our identity from God we will automatically try to get it from somewhere else. We need to learn to understand that what constitutes success in our society is not necessarily the same as God's unchanging view of success.

PRESENTATION THEMES

- Success in today's society is often linked to wealth and fame.

- Success in New Testament society was based on background and religious pedigree.

- Measured by contemporary standards of success, Jesus' life was a failure.

- Being faithful to our calling is the measure of success in God's eyes.

- Obedience to God's laws brings blessing, protection and strength.

> **Success in today's society is often linked to wealth and fame.**

The concept of success is defined by culture and peer group and has meant different things to different people at different times. The dictionary definition of 'success' is:

1. The favourable outcome of something attempted
2. The attainment of wealth and fame

The first definition is commonly accepted: achieving what you set out to accomplish or achieving your goals. The second definition is more revealing. It identifies wealth and fame as goals. In the West, these two things are so commonly sought that they are now incorporated into the very meaning of the word 'success'.

People will judge our success, the ads tell us, by the car we drive, the clothes we wear and the food we eat. If you see me driving a Mercedes, using a Gold American Express card or carrying Gucci luggage, you know that I am successful. Success is judged simply by the things you see. It has nothing to do with character or actions.

The result is that it is easy to be gripped by an urge to possess the symbols of success. Many push themselves deeper and deeper into debt and work longer and longer hours simply to get a better kitchen, a bigger house or the latest sound system.

As Rob Parsons has reminded us in his book *The Heart of Success*,[1] we need to consider not only the price of these things but the real cost in extra time spent on work to obtain the money to pay for them.

---

[1] Published by Hodder, 2002

'Toys Are Us'

One of the best examples of a successful life in many people's eyes was the American multi-millionaire Malcolm Forbes. Here are some facts:

- He owned eight homes including a 40 acre estate in New Jersey, a palace in Morocco, a chateau in France and an island in Fiji.
- He accumulated 2,200 paintings and 12 Russian Imperial Faberge eggs.
- His wealth was estimated to be somewhere between $400 million and $1.25 billion.
- His maxim was 'he who has the most toys wins.'
- He entertained royalty on his yacht.
- He jetted around in his private Boeing 727 named 'The Capitalist Tool'.
- He spent $2 million on a celebration of his seventieth birthday, flying guests from around the world to Morocco.

Forbes' definition of success was clear — 'he who has most toys wins.' In our society a person's success or significance or worth is equivalent to what they *have*.

Forbes stated in a TV interview, 'All I want to do is live long enough to enjoy all that I have.' Asked if he believed in life after death, he answered, 'Life after death will be no comparison to the life I am now living. I have the best possible life right now. It could never be any better.'

A few months later, Forbes died.

> **Success in New Testament society was based on background and religious pedigree.**

In the New Testament, success in Paul's culture meant having a good religious pedigree, being ultra-religious (a Pharisee) and demonstrating religious zeal. He was also highly educated and, by implication, from a good background.

In his culture, Paul was therefore a highly successful person. He had everything going for him, with enough of the icons of success of his culture to inspire envy in most other people.

However, Paul came to understand that success for him meant living a life which revolved around knowing Jesus and sharing his sufferings.

> I want to know Christ and the power of his resurrection and the fellowship of sharing in his sufferings, becoming like him in death, and so, somehow, to attain the resurrection from the dead.
>
> *Philippians 3:10–11*

This was a radically different set of priorities from those he pursued when, as Saul, he persecuted Christians.

> **Measured by contemporary standards
> of success, Jesus' life was a failure.**

According to the measures of success in New Testament times, Jesus' life did not fulfil the expectations of those around him. He did not have the background and religious pedigree of a Pharisee. Neither did he meet the expectations of a Jewish Messiah in the mould of a warrior king to lead God's people against Roman rule — a political leader who would inspire and motivate.

The survival of the Christian church more than 2000 years later is evidence that what Jesus taught did not die with him. The Holy Spirit made sure of that.

How should Christians, therefore, respond to the example of Jesus?

> **Being faithful to our calling is the
> measure of success in God's eyes.**

Success as a Christian is to do with exercising faith. Faith is much more than belief. It can be defined as taking God at his word. Real faith is demonstrated by actions.

> Now faith is being sure of what we hope for and certain of what
> we do not see. This is what the ancients were commended for.
> *Hebrews 11:1–2*

Hebrews 11 contains a list of Old Testament characters who are there because of their success in God's eyes. They were considered successful for being obedient to God, even before the life of Jesus.

Some of these people were rich and enjoyed great fame and wealth, for example Moses, Joseph, David and Abraham. These people certainly fit a Western definition of success. Success in God's eyes is therefore not necessarily incompatible with financial and economic success.

But we also find others in the list, for example Noah, who was ignored by his countrymen; and Rahab, who was a prostitute.

Some of the people listed are considered successful in spite of the fact that they did not live blameless lives. David, for example, committed murder and adultery. Moses committed murder.

What do these examples have in common? Simply this: all these people had faith in God that was worked out in their actions.

Successful Christians in God's eyes are ones who base real life decisions on what the Word of God says, when conventional behaviour tells them to do something else.

Multimedia Motivation

Richard Eyre, former Chief Executive of Pearson Television and ITV, had been prepared to give up his high profile job in advertising when he became a Christian. Working as media director in a major agency, he had recently made a re-commitment to Jesus, and was convinced that as a result he would have to become a 'full-time' church worker. He had got to the point of handing the company car back when someone at his church, who did not know him or his situation, had a specific word from God saying that someone who was about to give up their job should not do so. He stayed and eventually went on to develop his distinguished career in advertising and television. Richard says: 'My relationship with Jesus is my pearl of great price. I will not sacrifice it for anything.'

> ## Obedience to God's laws brings blessing, protection and strength.

God has established principles about how we should behave and live. It is clear that upholding these principles is a source of blessing. It was true for Joshua as he took on the responsibility of leading Israel after Moses died, and it is true for us today. God wants us to be successful and prosper in all we do.

Blessed is the man who does not walk in the counsel of the wicked or stand in the way of sinners or sit in the seat of mockers. But his delight is in the law of the LORD, and on his law he meditates day and night. He is like a tree planted by streams of water, which yields its fruit in season and whose leaf does not wither. Whatever he does prospers.

Psalm 1:1–3

Do not let this Book of the Law depart from your mouth; meditate on it day and night, so that you may be careful to do everything written in it. Then you will be prosperous and successful.

Joshua 1:8

Success is also linked to finding knowledge and wisdom.

The fear of the Lord is the beginning of wisdom, and knowledge of the Holy One is understanding.

Proverbs 9:10

We are reminded to follow this advice, regardless of our circumstances.

When you have eaten and are satisfied, praise the LORD your God for the good land he has given you. Be careful that you do not forget the LORD your God, failing to observe his commands, his laws and his decrees that I am giving you this day. Otherwise, when you eat and are satisfied, when you build fine houses and settle down, and when your herds and flocks grow large and your silver and gold increase and all you have is multiplied, then your heart will become proud and you will forget the LORD your God, who brought you out of Egypt, out of the land of slavery.

Deuteronomy 8:10–14

Prosperity and blessing are promised by God to those who follow his laws. There is no easy formula governing how we enjoy this blessing, but neither should prosperity only be measured in financial terms.

Death – the Acid Test

Death is the defining moment regarding our success. There is no more we can do.

This life is just a passing phase that will soon be over. Its only importance will lie in what it has achieved concerning the life to come. A bit like school examinations, they seem really important at the time, but once you have done them they provide a passport to the next thing and they then become almost totally unimportant.

Material success is a false idol, which will shape the thoughts, actions and choices of its followers. It is a trap set by Satan, especially for Christians with careers, especially for high earners. Those who allow themselves to get caught up in it will begin to judge life, people and events according to its demands and perspectives.

Satan's plan is to encourage a restlessness which will never satisfy. Some people will never get to a stage where they can assess the true value of what they are doing because they are too busy working their way up. Most people never get to the top — but, like the lottery, enough get there to convince the millions of others to spend their lives striving for it.

When you stand before God, will he say, 'Well done, good and faithful servant'? Isn't that the only thing that really matters?

Conclusion

Success in God's eyes is the outcome of knowing God's will for our lives as revealed in his word, and then being carefully obedient. It involves a whole change in the way we think. The results of this changed thinking will be different for each of us. We walk by faith, for example, when we:

- Pass over a business deal that does not have complete integrity

- Give away more money than we can afford

- Stick up for an underdog because it seems right in spite of opposition

- Genuinely seek God's will about whether to apply for a promotion

- Think long and hard about what car we drive

What is your definition of success? Is it success on the world's terms or is it to receive a 'Well done good and faithful servant' when you stand before God's throne at the end of your life?

> A certain ruler asked him (Jesus), "Good teacher, what must I do to inherit eternal life?"
>
> "...Sell everything you have and give to the poor, and you will have treasure in heaven. Then come and follow me." When he heard this, he became very sad, because he was a man of great wealth. Jesus looked at him and said, "How hard it is for the rich to enter the kingdom of God!"
>
> *Luke 18:18–24*

This is tough teaching — many never grasp it, including the rich young ruler for whom the choice between wealth and eternal life was too much.

Cartoon Conundrum

At a time when his business was in severe financial trouble, a friend got a call from the marketing director of an influential publishing company. She asked him to do a joint presentation to a third party to acquire the rights to launch a magazine and run a fan club for a very popular children's cartoon character.

The problem was that, as a Christian, he believed the cartoon character in question was a bad influence on some children. Yet to turn down the opportunity not only risked damaging his relationship with the publishing company but also missing out on a very large revenue opportunity which he desperately needed.

After prayerful consideration, he arranged to meet his contact at the publishing company and explained to her his reservations, that he did not wish to proceed with the proposal and why this was. He was surprised by her response: 'Well, if it's as damaging as you say, I can understand why you don't want to run a fan club. Perhaps we shouldn't do a magazine — I'll talk to the MD about it.'

To date the cartoon character in question still has no official fan club and no magazine and there are no plans to launch them — a highly unlikely but very pleasing result for my colleague. And his relationship with the influential publishing company is in very good shape. God is faithful!

QUESTIONS FOR STUDY

1. Look at Paul's list of achievements in Philippians 3:5-6. Make a list of things in your own life that you have been given or have achieved that make you feel successful.

2. What are your career goals? And your life goals?

3. Is it wrong to want to get to the top? How far would you go to achieve 'the top' in whatever career you are in?

4. What feelings do you have when you think about your death? If you knew you were to die next month, how would you spend the time?

5. Is it possible to 'live by faith' in your job? Can you give some examples?

6. Jesus said, 'Do not store up for yourselves treasures on earth... but store up for yourselves treasures in heaven' (Matthew 6:19–20) and, 'where your treasure is, there your heart will be also.' How far have you accepted the world's view of success?

7. Look through the Gospels, and notice how Jesus did not go primarily to those who were successful in society's eyes, but deliberately concentrated on the poor, the sick and the outcast. Do you measure people by what they have or appear to have?

Chapter Four

MANAGING TIME

Be very careful, then, how you live — not as unwise but as wise, making the most of every opportunity, because the days are evil. Therefore do not be foolish, but understand what the Lord's will is.

Ephesians 5:15–17

INTRODUCTION

The time we have to serve the Lord in this life is short, deceptively short. We are instructed to be 'very careful' how we live and we are to 'make the most of every opportunity'. This chapter will help us understand God's priorities for our lives.

Often we get stuck in unhelpful patterns of behaviour and do not have the motivation to make the changes that would help us make better use of our time. Proper biblical convictions about time can help to give us the urgency and motivation to make these changes.

PRESENTATION THEMES

- God wants us to plan with him how we use the time he has given us.

- God knows our need for balanced lives, and has established guidelines to follow.

- We receive insight from God about our lives when we take time to be still before him.

- Life choices have consequences which we need to think through with God.

- Jesus' awareness of his life, purpose and times is an example we need to model.

> **God wants us to plan with him how
> we use the time he has given us.**

We are accountable to God for the lives he has given us, and will be answerable to him for our lives when we die. This is the idea of stewardship.

God is therefore interested in working with us as a friend and partner. He wants us to enjoy the unique opportunities for service which he offers in his world. Planning our lives with God is therefore something which he encourages, since he knows what is best for us. We need actively to bring God into our decision-making.

> To man belong the plans of the heart, but from the Lord comes the reply of the tongue.
>
> Commit to the Lord whatever you do, and your plans will succeed.
>
> In his heart a man plans his course, but the Lord determines his steps.
>
> *Proverbs 16:1, 3 & 9*

We also have a past, which we are powerless to change, retrieve or repeat. Decisions made and actions taken have consequences which we may have to face. However, the truth of the gospel is that by faith in Christ, our sins (things we do in disobedience of God) are no longer remembered by him, and that Christ's history becomes our history. Our future is unknown to us, but clear to God.

> All the days ordained for me were written in your book before one of them came to be.
>
> *Psalm 139:16*

We are being arrogant if we plan out our own lives without reference to God, and this can extend to our ambitions for any business venture we are involved with.

> Now listen, you who say, "Today or tomorrow we will go to this or that city, spend a year there, carry on business and make money." Why, you do not even know what will happen tomorrow....
>
> *James 4:13–14*

The only thing we can be certain about our lives is that one day they will end.

God knows our need for balanced lives, and has established guidelines to follow.

> Let there be lights in the expanse of the sky to separate the day from the night, and let them serve as signs to mark seasons and days and years....
>
> *Genesis 1:14*

God is the creator of time. Within the movement of time he has established cycles. There are seasonal, yearly, weekly and daily cycles which we use to measure time passing.

> Remember the Sabbath day by keeping it holy. Six days you shall labour and do all your work, but the seventh day is a Sabbath to the LORD your God. On it, you shall not do any work....
>
> *Exodus 20:8–10*

As part of his creation, God establishes the Sabbath principle — a day of rest — as an important guideline for achieving a balanced life. We all need to recognise the value of understanding and applying these cycles of time to our lives. God reflects on his own creative activity to observe what has been achieved to date.

> By the seventh day God had finished the work he had been doing; so on the seventh day he rested from all his work. And God blessed the seventh day and made it holy, because on it he rested from all the work of creating that he had done.
>
> *Genesis 2:2–3*

The model God set up — of working on six days and resting on the seventh — establishes the necessity for rest and worship, as well as forbidding idleness. In managing our time we need to preserve the conviction that we must keep one day in seven distinct from work.

God's cycles extend to how we behave on a daily basis. Jesus encourages us to enjoy each day for what it is: a unique event in time which will never be repeated. If we are planning our lives with God, we should only concern ourselves with today's troubles.

> Therefore do not worry about tomorrow, for tomorrow will worry about itself. Each day has enough trouble of its own.
>
> *Matthew 6:34*

In relationships, the New Testament teaches that some things must be settled today so that bitterness and resentment are not given an opportunity to grow.

> "In your anger do not sin": Do not let the sun go down while you are still angry, and do not give the devil a foothold.
>
> *Ephesians 4:26–27*

Choosing the right time to do what we do is also something we need to learn. We need to learn to enjoy working to God's cycles, as the writer of Ecclesiastes puts it.

> There is a time for everything,
> and a season for every activity under heaven:
> a time to be born and a time to die,

a time to plant and a time to uproot,
a time to kill and a time to heal,
a time to tear down and a time to build,
a time to weep and a time to laugh,
a time to mourn and a time to dance,
a time to scatter stones and a time to gather them,
a time to embrace and a time to refrain,
a time to search and a time to give up,
a time to keep and a time to throw away,
a time to tear and a time to mend,
a time to be silent and a time to speak,
a time to love and a time to hate,
a time for war and a time for peace.

Ecclesiastes 3:1–8

Choosing to Balance

'I would happily give up half my salary if I could work half the time', said a derivatives specialist from a leading American investment bank on a recent flight between London and New York. 'I am missing seeing my young family grow up. My wife and I have every material blessing we could ever want, but we would prefer a less disruptive lifestyle. However, my company would never accept such a proposal. They would just fire me and replace me with someone else. What options do I have?'

It is often the fear of change that prevents us from taking action. It takes courage to overcome fear. The alternative can be a paralysis which affects all our waking moments, and grips us with uncertainty.

In Christ, we can enjoy the freedom to tackle fear, and change.

> **We receive insight from God about our lives when we take time to be still before him.**

The Bible tells us clearly again and again that putting time with God at the top of our agenda is the best way to live our lives.

> Be still before the Lord and wait patiently for him; do not fret when men succeed in their ways, when they carry out their wicked schemes.
>
> *Psalm 37:7*

> Be still, and know that I am God; I will be exalted among the nations, I will be exalted in the earth.
>
> *Psalm 46:10*

> But seek first his kingdom and his righteousness, and all these things will be given to you as well.
>
> *Matthew 6:33*

Many of us, soon after waking up, start firing on all cylinders, and keep the pace up all day until we collapse, exhausted, into bed. There is nothing wrong with being busy. After all we are creative, skilful people in a world God wants us to enjoy. But the temptation of being busy is that we can ignore God. Martin Luther wrote in his diary that he was so busy at a particular time that he had to get up *two hours earlier* so that he could pray more. Luther understood that it is God who gets things done, not us working in our own strength.

The importance of prayer as a foundation for how to spend our time is addressed by Bill Hybels in his book *Too Busy Not To Pray*:

> Authentic Christians are persons who stand apart from others, even other Christians, as though listening to a different

drummer. Their character seems deeper, their ideas fresher, their spirit softer, their courage greater, their leadership stronger, their concerns wider, their compassion more genuine, their convictions more concrete. Embarrassingly, few Christians ever reach this level of authenticity; most are just too busy. And the arch-enemy of spiritual authenticity is busyness, which is closely tied to something the Bible calls worldliness; getting caught up with this society's agenda, objectives and activities to the neglect of walking with God.[1]

(p. 100)

Those of us who discover this secret, and apply it, are people whom God can really use.

> ## Life choices have consequences which we need to think through with God.

It is important that we allow the Holy Spirit to set our priorities, by regularly spending time with him, and specific-ally asking for guidance.

Generally speaking, the Bible places greater priority on family life than work. This should be reflected in how we order our lives as Christians, as we trust God rather than excessively long hours to provide for our needs.

Of course, there will be times when we need to spend longer than usual at work. We may be required to dedicate all our energies to important tasks to which it is quite possible we have been called by God. Some jobs require extremely committed people who will put in long hours because of the responsibilities involved. Christians should not be afraid of taking on such roles, provided the consequences have been thought through. God may want to develop our talents through such assignments.

---

[1] *Too Busy Not to Pray* Bill Hybels © Published by IVP & UCCF Used by permission.

However, it is when these times become frequent, or excessively prolonged, that alarm bells should ring and we should urgently come before the Lord, as well as wise Christian friends, for guidance.

Of course, life consists of a variety of competing activities to which we cannot devote our energies equally all of the time — marriage/family, career, education, church, recreation. There are necessarily phases in our lives which reflect the cycles instituted by God in his creation. Whatever we do, God's intent is that we depend on him for our needs.

Each one of us has an inclination to give too much time to some things, and too little time to others. We need to consider the claim of each, work out our priorities before God, and ensure that nothing important is neglected.

Marriage and Family

All relationships need time to develop and grow, and marriage has a high place in God's plan for his people. Marriage is therefore a commitment which needs to be taken seriously. A direct consequence of choosing to get married or have a family is that we will need to be even more careful about how we share our time between different activities.

Meeting basic needs through income, companionship, nurture of children and care for the elderly are all choices which have to be worked out on a daily basis.

> If anyone does not provide for his relatives, and especially for his immediate family, he has denied the faith and is worse than an unbeliever.
>
> *I Timothy 5:8*

Career

For a Christian, building a career can be a legitimate part of our God-given calling. However, it must continue to be inspired so that it does not displace other priorities. There is no mention of 'career' in the Bible, and it is not a right to which we are entitled.

Education

The opportunity to develop knowledge and new skills is God-given, and should be taken and used diligently. God has given us talents which we are encouraged to discover. Mid-life study, for example, is one way of pursuing this objective. It is normally done at the cost of other priorities, because of the amount of time and energy that it takes up.

Church

Active involvement in a church is a requirement of faith. Being 'active' includes, for example, gathering regularly for worship, fellowship, and prayer. It can also extend to some specific aspect of ministry or service. In this respect, a believer may have additional demands on his/her energies and time over and above that experienced by people who are not part of a church. However, God always gives us the strength to carry out what he wants us to do.

> Let us not give up meeting together, as some are in the habit of doing, but let us encourage one another....
> *Hebrews 10:25*

> It was he who gave some to be apostles, some to be prophets, some to be evangelists, and some to be pastors and teachers, to prepare God's people for works of service, so that the body of Christ may be built up....
> *Ephesians 4:11–13*

The choice of ministry or service, as well as where it is worked out, will not always focus on the church organisation. It may include works of service in a business, a company, a school, a hospital, surgery or home – provided it is consistent with the calling which God has revealed.

Recreation

God rested after his creation. We, too, are designed for rest. We need to make time for relaxation, exercise, socialising and hobbies, all of which have an important place.

> **Jesus' awareness of his life, purpose and times is an example we need to model.**

Jesus' ministry lasted approximately three years, from the age of thirty to thirty-three. During this time, he demonstrated a clear focus on fulfilling certain tasks and choosing to do what he wanted to do when he was ready. He was not hurried by those around him. His actions display a sense of purpose, and understanding of what he was called to do.

Therefore Jesus told them, "The right time for me has not yet come; for you any time is right.... You go to the Feast. I am not yet going up to this Feast, because for me the right time has not yet come."

John 7:6–8

On various occasions, Jesus retreated to quiet places to pray, so that he could continue to discern what it was his Father wanted him to do.

Very early in the morning, while it was still dark, Jesus got up, left the house and went off to a solitary place, where he prayed. Simon and his companions went to look for him, and when they found him, they exclaimed: "Everyone is looking for you!" Jesus replied, "Let us go somewhere else—to the nearby villages—so I can preach there also. That is why I have come."

Mark 1:35–38

Achieving a similar sense of purpose and understanding about our own place in God's plan is something to which we should all aspire.

Conclusion

Authentic Christianity is not about doctrines — it is about a relationship with God. It is a supernatural walk with a living, dynamic, communicating God, who chooses to speak to us on a regular basis. However, we need to listen if we are to know how to make best use of the opportunities presented to us in our short lives on earth.

A key part of being an authentic follower of Jesus is, therefore, spending quality time with our Father God. He wants to give us our hearts' desire. He wants to speak to us about the things that we are concerned about. He wants to teach us how to grow in faith.

As a general principle, God will not ask us to do more than we can physically do. If we are constantly struggling to fit everything in, we need to ask him to show us why, and look at what needs to change.

Personal circumstances and personal stamina will always differ. This means that some people will have more liberty than others to determine how much of their day is taken up with work, recreation, family and church. We need to trust God for his provision in each situation.

QUESTIONS FOR STUDY

1. What are your major areas of responsibility? Rank them in order of importance. Is this reflected in the time you give to these things?

2. What are your priorities? How much can we choose what we do? When are you at your best in the day? Plan to use this time for important things.

3. Have you an overall plan for your life? Like management/time planning 'gurus' — where do you want to be in five years time and what do you have to do to get there? Should everyone have such a plan? Is this 'Christian'? (Look at James 4:13–15)

4. What should we be considering in planning and progressing our careers? How should such planning fit in with our responsibilities to our family? To our church?

5. If God wants you to do something, will he provide the time — like other resources?

6. Do you always/ever have a sense of rushing around? Is this a Christian way of doing things? (Look at Psalm 46:10) What is the answer to this?

7. Why is it difficult to wait on God — for *his* time? God's time scale is different from ours. (Look at Psalm 90:4). He works in different ways and at a different speed. (Look at Exodus 14:10–14 & Psalm 37:7.)

8. How do you divide up your time in a week....
    How much time for work? For family? For leisure?
    For God?

9. 'Seven whole days not one in seven I will praise Thee.'
    Where and how does this worship come in everyday
    things? (Look at Romans 12:1–2.) How are the
    ordinary things of daily life to be turned into worship?
    Just the way we do things —quality? Or is there more
    to it?

10. What should Sunday be like? What should we do and
     not do? (Look at Mark 2:23–28.)

Chapter Five

HANDLING MONEY

Honour the LORD with your wealth, with the firstfruits of all your crops; then your barns will be filled to overflowing, and your vats will brim over with new wine.

Proverbs 3:9–10

INTRODUCTION

Money and work are closely linked. We all need to earn some to live; we may need to manage our investments, and we all need to plan for our future and families.

However, our attitude to money is a test of how faithful we are to God, and how much we really trust him for what we need. Martin Luther wrote that there were three conversions necessary to see the kingdom of God — the conversion of the heart, the mind and the purse.

It is the last of these that is often so difficult, particularly for people who live in a Western society where we have learned to rely more on the market economy than on God for day to day needs.

As Christians we already have all the security we could possibly want —we just have to realise it! This chapter helps us to understand the nature of money and formulate some practical principles by which to live.

PRESENTATION THEMES

- Money is a necessary part of our society. It is neither good nor bad. It is neutral.

- Jesus teaches that our wealth is not our own. We look after it for God.

- God has established the principle of giving to ensure we rely on him for all our needs.

- The desire for (and the possession of) money is a seductive source of false security.

> **Money is a necessary part of our society.
> It is neither good nor bad. It is neutral.**

There is no implication in the Bible that money, or making money, is evil. Money is simply a convenient tool that simplifies trade. In his book *Champions for God at Work*, David Kellett outlines its usefulness:

> Money, as such, is not an evil: it pays for the things we need. It is essential if we are going to support those who depend on us. It also means that we can have some of the enjoyable things of life, such as a holiday, and it gives us the opportunity to be generous to others....

However, our attitude towards money — how we earn it, how we spend it, how we give it away — is right at the heart of our faith and Jesus had a lot to say about it.

> As Jesus started on his way, a man ran up to him and fell on his knees before him. "Good teacher," he asked, "what must I do to inherit eternal life?"
>
> "....You know the commandments: 'Do not murder, do not commit adultery, do not steal, do not give false testimony, do not defraud, honour your father and mother.'"
>
> "Teacher," he declared, "all these I have kept since I was a boy."
>
> Jesus looked at him and loved him. "One thing you lack," he said. "Go, sell everything you have and give to the poor, and you will have treasure in heaven. Then come, follow me."
>
> At this the man's face fell. He went away sad, because he had great wealth.

Jesus looked around and said to his disciples, "How hard it is for the rich to enter the kingdom of God!" The disciples were amazed at his words. But Jesus said again, "Children, how hard it is to enter the kingdom of God! It is easier for a camel to go through the eye of a needle than for a rich man to enter the kingdom of God."

Mark 10:17–25

So what principles can we learn to live by?

Jesus teaches that our wealth is not our own. We look after it for God.

Our ability to earn a living, and generate wealth, flows from the talents and skills which we have all been given by God. The idea of looking after what God has given us, and making the most of it, is the heart of stewardship. Stewardship applies to our money and wealth as much as to other gifts and abilities we have, for which we will ultimately be accountable.

Take the talent from him and give it to the one who has the ten talents. For everyone who has will be given more, and he will have an abundance. Whoever does not have, even what he has will be taken from him.

Matthew 25:28–29

Since the indirect source of any wealth is therefore God, we need to sustain an attitude of thankfulness to him for all we require, in the good times as well as the bad.

You may say to yourself, "My power and the strength of my hands have produced this wealth for me." But remember the Lord your God, for it is he who gives you the ability to produce wealth, and so confirms his covenant, which he swore to your forefathers, as it is today.

Deuteronomy 8:17–18

Are we therefore entitled to 'own' anything at all?

There are at least three different discipleship situations identified in the New Testament:

- Those people who left everything because following Jesus involved them specifically in an itinerant lifestyle (the Twelve).
- Those people who retained possession of homes and other goods which were used for the sake of the kingdom.
- Those people who needed to sell all their possessions as an act of repentance because they had become a god (for example, the rich young ruler).

Though Jesus called some people to sell everything they owned, it is clear that this was not required of all his disciples. There are no fixed rules for how to respond to how our wealth should be used. But we must choose always to ask God to reveal to us how he wants us to use what he has entrusted to us.

Everything comes from you, and we have given you only what comes from your hand.

I Chronicles 29:14b

We need to hold what we have been given lightly, responsibly and joyfully.

Constructing the Kingdom

John Laing, founder of the building company, worked out his personal system for giving before God when he was 27, and facing bankruptcy. He kept to it all his life, and he gave away just about everything. He built up a multi-million pound business. When he died, his estate was valued at just £347.

> **God has established the principle of giving,
> to ensure we rely on him for our needs.**

God has instituted giving as a way of showing his blessing. Jesus said that it is more blessed to give than to receive. Giving is associated with returning to God a part, indeed the best part, of what has been produced or earned, as a sign of the gratitude and respect to a loving creator God.

> Honour the LORD with your wealth, with the firstfruits of all your crops; then your barns will be filled to overflowing, and your vats will brim over with new wine.
>
> *Proverbs 3:9–10*

How does giving bless us?

- It gives God an opportunity to be God, a provider of what we need
- We can see God move miraculously
- Our faith will grow as a result of obedience

There are some core principles about how we should give out of what God gives us.

Generously

> Remember this: Whoever sows sparingly will also reap sparingly, and whoever sows generously will also reap generously.
>
> *II Corinthians 9:6*

Systematically and Proportionately

> On the first day of every week, each one of you should set aside a sum of money in keeping with his income, saving it up, so that when I come no collections will have to be made.
>
> *I Corinthians 16:2*

Joyfully and Voluntarily

Each man should give what he has decided in his heart to give, not reluctantly or under compulsion, for God loves a cheerful giver.

II Corinthians 9:7

Sacrificially

Out of the most severe trial, their overflowing joy and extreme poverty welled up in rich generosity. For I testify that they gave as much as they were able, and even beyond their ability.

II Corinthians 8:2–3

Quietly and Discreetly

Be careful not to do your 'acts of righteousness' before men, to be seen by them. If you do, you will have no reward from your Father in heaven.... But when you give to the needy, do not let your left hand know what your right hand is doing, so that your giving may be in secret. Then your Father, who sees what is done in secret, will reward you.

Matthew 6:1, 3–4

It is very easy indeed to deceive ourselves in the area of giving. The consequences can be severe — a curse instead of a blessing.

Will a man rob God? Yet you rob me. But you ask, 'How do we rob you?' In tithes and offerings. You are under a curse — the whole nation of you — because you are robbing me. Bring the whole tithe into the storehouse, that there may be food in my house. Test me in this, says the LORD Almighty, and see if I will not throw open the floodgates of heaven and pour out so much blessing that you will not have room enough for it.

Malachi 3:8–10

God invites our obedience. The principle is that it is our duty to take the firstfruits of our labour — here 10%, or the tithe—and give them to God. This is a very simple and clear instruction but one we tend to ignore or explain away, because it is hard. It is easy to convince ourselves that we cannot afford it.

That is precisely the point. If you can afford it, where is the faith? God wants us to test him, so that we will be blessed. If you have never known what it is like to give when you cannot afford it, you can really miss out, because you will not see what miracles God will do. There is only one way to find out.

Chocolate Money

George Cadbury, the man who founded Cadbury's, was passionate in his dislike for hoarding money, and he gave huge sums away — in doing so he revolutionised the treatment of workers in this country, and helped many Christian ventures. He determined also not to leave any large sums to his children, believing that money would be most unhelpful to their development as Christians.

As A. G. Gardiner pointed out in his *Life of George Cadbury* (Cassell, 1923), he saw business not as an end in itself, but as a means to an end, a way he could do things which were really important. These included caring for others, missionary work and fighting injustices, such as the terrible exploitation of child chimney sweeps.

> # The desire for and the possession of money is a seductive source of false security.

The temptation that faces us all is to look for security the way the world does. This can include trying to store up assets to make sure that if times turn bad we have enough left to tide us over. Maybe we are looking forward to the time when we will be 'financially secure'. The danger is that we can depend too much on our house and bank accounts.

Jesus was quite clear that trying to find security apart from God is harmful and completely unnecessary.

> Then he said to them, "Watch out! Be on your guard against all kinds of greed; a man's life does not consist in the abundance of his possessions."
>
> *Luke 12:15*

> "Do not store up for yourselves treasures on earth, where moth and rust destroy, and where thieves break in and steal. But store up for yourselves treasures in heaven, where moth and rust do not destroy, and where thieves do not break in and steal."
>
> *Matthew 6:19–20*

There is no ambiguity. Jesus states it is simply impossible to serve both God and money. Getting our attitude to money right is therefore fundamental to God, and can impact his giving us significant ministry responsibility elsewhere.

> No servant can serve two masters. Either he will hate the one and love the other, or he will be devoted to the one and despise the other. You cannot serve both God and Money."
>
> *Luke 16:13 and Matthew 6:24*

Either you learn to trust God with your money and use it in his service, or you do not — there is no half way position.

Either your life is dictated by what you can afford, what *you* think is sensible, or it is dictated by what God is telling you. (Which frequently can make no sense, according to conventional wisdom!)

Jesus taught that God knows our heart better than we do ourselves. We need to be aware of complacency in money matters.

So, is it wrong to desire to become wealthy? The desire to become wealthy for its own sake leads to spiritual exposure and unwise choices. It can allow salary alone to determine career or job choice rather than a balanced assessment of life priorities.

> People who want to get rich fall into temptation and a trap and into many foolish and harmful desires that plunge men into ruin and destruction. For the love of money is a root of all kinds of evil. Some people, eager for money, have wandered from the faith and pierced themselves with many griefs.
>
> *I Timothy 6: 9–10*

And yet, in Western economies, it is likely that people will become wealthy. The Protestant work ethic is known to generate prosperity: *If* we are educated, employed, and own a home and a car, then we are wealthy from an historical and a worldwide perspective.

It is therefore even more important that we understand the trappings of wealth, and be prepared for them, since they can represent a barrier to understanding God's kingdom and his planned blessings for us.

Conclusion

Ultimately, money cannot buy life. We cannot take our investments, goods and properties with us when we die, and should therefore hold onto them lightly, albeit managed in a responsible and accountable way while we can. Anyone who does not take this attitude is described by God as a fool:

> "The ground of a certain rich man produced a good crop. He thought to himself, `What shall I do? I have no place to store my crops.'
>
> "Then he said, `This is what I'll do. I will tear down my barns and build bigger ones, and there I will store all my grain and my goods. And I'll say to myself, "You have plenty of good things laid up for many years. Take life easy; eat, drink and be merry"'
>
> "But God said to him, `You fool! This very night your life will be demanded from you. Then who will get what you have prepared for yourself?'
>
> "This is how it will be with anyone who stores up things for himself but is not rich towards God."
>
> *Luke 12:16–21*

The positive alternative offered by Jesus is:

> Therefore I tell you, do not worry about your life, what you will eat or drink; or about your body, what you will wear. Is not life more important than food, and the body more important than clothes?
>
> *Matthew 6:25*

If we are constantly worrying about how we are going to pay the mortgage or whether or not we are going to be made redundant, these thoughts will consume our waking hours and we will not be much use for anything else.

Jesus says our Father knows what we need and will provide it. We have to make up our minds to trust him with this promise. If we are looking to please our Father, everything else will be taken care of.

QUESTIONS FOR STUDY

1. Is it wrong to be wealthy? Is it wrong to desire to be wealthy?

2. Can we recognise when we have 'enough'? Is this helpful or not in determining how to use the talents God has given us?

3. What are the principles for guiding us in the use of our wealth? For example, should we set limits to our personal expenditure?

4. What is a reasonable balance of spending/consumption versus giving for Christians in the Western world? In Western society, what is a realistic 21st century tithe?

5. What sacrifices are we prepared to make to become wealthy (e.g. ambitions)?

6. How should we honour God in the spending/budgeting of other people's money (e.g. business, charity, school)?

7. How legitimate is speculation as a means of wealth creation?

8. How should we handle the responsibilities of risk? How are risk and faith connected?

9. How should your church set its priorities for spending? For example, is it better to spend money on a new piano, a part-time youth worker or re-pointing the brickwork on the 17th century church steeple?

Chapter Six

COPING WITH STRESS

Do not be anxious about anything, but in everything, by prayer and petition, with thanksgiving, present your requests to God. And the peace of God which transcends all understanding will guard your hearts and minds in Christ Jesus.

Philippians 4: 4–7

INTRODUCTION

In our society there is more and more mention of stress and stress-related illness, particularly related to the workplace. While 'stress' is not a term used in the Bible, the concepts that come closest to describing the same experience are 'testing' and 'anxiety', about which the Bible has a great deal to say.

Some of the stresses in our society can be alleviated by adopting biblical principles for our lives. For Christians, this can result from learning to understand God's priorities for our life and trust him to bring about his will, rather than working in our own strength. This is, of course, easy to write, hard to put into practice.

Christians are likely to face additional pressures as we cope, firstly, with spiritual attack, and secondly, with the additional demands of church life. However, we can respond to both, provided we understand God's purposes and resources better.

PRESENTATION THEMES

- Stress is a human reality which existed in biblical times as well as today.
- People have differing abilities to cope with stress in their lives.
- Stress can be caused by failing to practise God's principles in our lives.
- God's promises do not change, in spite of how we feel. How we cope with stress will depend on the discipline of time spent with God.

> **Stress is a human reality which existed in biblical times as well as today.**

A dictionary definition of 'stress' describes it as mental, emotional, or physical strain or tension. In physics, it is also described as a force which produces deformation or strain. It is a strain that something or someone is required to bear, that tests that thing or person's capacity to bear it.

In physics, stress is a problem only when it exceeds the capacity of the component to bear it. In physical structures, components are designed to handle anticipated stresses. For example, an elevated motorway is designed for the considerable stress of fast moving cars. However, when such a structure is hit by an earthquake, as happened in Kobe or Los Angeles, the concrete legs of the motorway can snap. Here the structure was stressed beyond its design limits and collapsed.

Stress in people works on a similar principle. We are inevitably exposed to strains in our daily lives, some of which we can cope with, some of which will be too much for us.

In biblical times, concerns about the future were no different from today. Economic and political uncertainty caused people to worry. Jesus spoke to this natural human characteristic on multiple occasions:

> Therefore I tell you, do not worry about your life, what you will eat or drink; or about your body, what you will wear. Is not life more important than food, the body more important than clothes? ...Who of you by worrying can add a single hour to his life?

> *Matthew 6:25 & 27*

Therefore do not worry about tomorrow, for tomorrow will worry about itself. Each day will have enough trouble of its own.

Matthew 6:34

Martha, Martha, you are worried and upset about many things, but only one thing is needed. Mary has chosen what is better, and it will not be taken away from her.

Luke 10: 41–42

Jesus' emphasis was on recognising that God's love cannot be contained by human timescales and activities. To worry about things over which we have no control prevents us from seeing God at work. We are to plan responsibly with God, but to leave the outcomes with him.

**People have differing abilities to
cope with stress in their lives.**

We are all different, and God has made us that way. It is therefore not surprising that we respond to stress in different ways. We need to know what we are capable of handling, and to recognise the signs when we are overdoing it.

Some people thrive on last-minute deadlines, juggling multiple projects, managing the responsibilities of large budgets.... Not all bad, in itself, but only when it is incessant and there is no relief.

Because God has made us different, there is no one single way to respond to stress. What is overload for one person may be welcome stimulation for another, depending on our respective abilities and experience.

There are also differences within one person about capacity to handle stress, depending on the occasion. Today you may be able to cope with a particular situation, but tomorrow it may be too much. What may be overwhelming stress at one time of your life may be easy later on when you have acquired the necessary skills and experience.

Stress can be caused by failing to practise God's principles in our lives.

Sources of stress are many and varied. But among them can be included the various topics considered in this book where we have identified clear biblical principles and attitudes about who we are in Christ, and our unique place in God's kingdom. These should give us confidence to root our lives in the truth of our unique identity, and help equip us to cope with the pressures that we face.

God's View of Work

- God intended us to work. Reconcile yourself to this fact.
- There is dignity in all kinds of work. Do not despise what God has given you to do.
- Remain within your calling. Do not settle for something that is under-stimulating, and do not overreach yourself for glamorous employment which is unsuited to your talents.
- Work at a job that is honourable, and that you can do with a good conscience.
- Work for reward from God.

Time

- Be diligent and rest. Laziness and over-commitment both lead to stress.
- Find time for all your priorities, and do not neglect any of them (God, family, work, exercise). The guilt attached to neglected priorities alone will create stress.
- Procrastination and living in chaos because of failure to plan will create stress.

Money

- Desiring to be wealthy will create its own pressures.
- Be generous in helping others with your money —concern for other people is a great antidote to stress and anxiety.
- Avoid excessive debt which you have no possibility of repaying.

Operating Outside our Calling

> For we are God's workmanship, created in Christ Jesus to do good works, which God prepared in advance for us to do.
>
> *Ephesians 2:10*

God has given each one of us different gifts, and prepared in advance special roles and responsibilities for us all. This may cover different areas of our lives: family, job, church or community. If we do not know what these things are, or we ignore what God has told us, we are likely to:

- Take on much more than God wants us to
- Operate out of a sense of drivenness or guilt rather than calling
- Do things where there is no spiritual blessing
- Be working solely in our own strength, which is a waste of time
- Doubt whether what we are doing is right

Failure to Spend Time with God

> Be still before the LORD and wait patiently for him;
>> do not fret when men succeed in their ways,
>>> when they carry out their wicked schemes.

Psalm 37:7

> Be still, and know that I am God;
>> I will be exalted among the nations,
>>> I will be exalted in the earth.

Psalm 46:1

We are all called to 'be still' before God —without exception. This is an essential discipline for spiritual growth, for which there are no shortcuts. We all think we are different, that our jobs demand more, and that we are more in control, but that is not true. Of course, some of us sometimes have to spend more time at work, and have more demanding deadlines and bigger responsibilities.

We can keep going for a long time simply by filling our life with activity, but this pattern ultimately leads to exhaustion and burn-out.

God is always with us. We have to learn how to depend on him.

> Unless the Lord builds the house,
>> its builders labour in vain.
> Unless the Lord watches over the city,
>> the watchmen stand guard in vain.
> In vain you rise early and stay up late,
>> toiling for food to eat —
> for he grants sleep to those he loves.

Psalm 127:1–2

Jesus did not do everything himself. Neither are we expected to. He chose how he used his time, including making time to 'be still' before his Father. So must we.

Learn from Paul's example.

If you think your life is full of stressful circumstances, consider Paul's.....

> Five times I received from the Jews the forty lashes minus one. Three times I was beaten with rods, once I was stoned, three times I was shipwrecked, I spent a night and a day in the open sea, I have been constantly on the move. I have been in danger from rivers, in danger from bandits, in danger from my own countrymen, in danger from Gentiles; in danger in the city, in danger in the country, in danger at sea; and in danger from false brothers. I have laboured and toiled and have often gone without sleep; I have known hunger and thirst and have often gone without food; I have been cold and naked. Besides everything else, I face daily the pressure of my concern for all the churches.
>
> *II Corinthians 11:24–28*

**God's promises do not change,
in spite of how we feel.**

We need to trust God for the outcomes of what we are trying to do, and ask him to help us let go of our anxieties.

How can we trust God rather than being buffeted by circumstances?

Jesus warned his disciples that they would suffer difficulties on account of being his followers. However, he also promised the Holy Spirit to equip them and give them peace. We are all entitled to this same promise in Christ.

> I have told you these things, so that in me you may have peace. In this world you will have trouble. But take heart! I have overcome the world.
>
> *John 16:33*

At the same time, we must expect spiritual opposition if we are doing what God has called us to do. Living life through grace can therefore be a stressful experience if we try and do it alone.

> For our struggle is not against flesh and blood, but against the rulers, against the authorities, against the powers of this dark world and against the spiritual forces of evil in the heavenly realms.

Ephesians 6:12

Perception is Everything

Why is it that two people can be subject to the same degree of stress and one flourishes while the other falls apart?

Let us consider one stressful situation: the Israelites versus the Philistines in I Samuel 17. The Israelite army is completely overwhelmed by the prospect of fighting Goliath. But young David comes along, says, "Who is this uncircumcised Philistine that he should defy the armies of the living God?" —pulls out his catapult, and kills him.

They were confronted with exactly the same situation — yet the soldiers were anxious, while David remained calm. The difference? Simply that the soldiers saw the giant in relation to themselves while David saw the giant in relation to God. Which of them saw the situation as it really was? David did. The truth was that the Israelite army had no valid reason to be fearful —they had the living God on their side. And so do you.

We are not so much affected by our circumstances as by how we perceive them and whether we rely on God to inspire us. What or who is your 'Goliath' today?

> **How we cope with stress will depend on
> the discipline of time spent with God.**

Being a Christian does not guarantee a life free from things that can cause stress. But Christians can and should be free of its negative effects. It is wrong to believe that all our stress would go away if we could only change our circumstances. There are some things, many things, that are simply impossible to change.

Most often it is we ourselves who need to change, including our attitudes and our capacity to cope. It can be for this very purpose that the Lord has introduced these circumstances into our lives.

Stress presents an opportunity to grow, to increase in our spiritual capacity to cope and to gain experience so that what seemed impossible to cope with at first can now be handled.

Paul's words in Philippians 4 give some clear guidance as to how we may go about this:

> Rejoice in the Lord always. I will say it again. Rejoice. Let your gentleness be evident to all. The Lord is near. Do not be anxious about anything, but in everything, by prayer and petition, with thanksgiving, present your requests to God. And the peace of God which transcends all understanding will guard your hearts and minds in Christ Jesus.
>
> *Philippians 4: 4–7*

Put into practice what you know to be true

'Rejoice' (v. 4), 'Let your gentleness be evident to all' (v. 5) and, 'Do not be anxious' (v. 6), are all commands. But they are easier said than done! The answer is not so much to try harder to obey these commands, but to focus on believing the truth: 'The Lord is near' (v. 5). When we understand that this is really true, it will make all the difference.

- Then there will be a gentleness of spirit that is evident to others, rather than a moody lashing out; blaming, and resenting circumstances, other people, and God.

- There will be rejoicing in place of anxiety.

Pray to God

- We are invited to pray about everything (v. 6).
  Our prayers are not to be confined to so-called spiritual subjects, e.g. for the Lord's help in preparing our Sunday School lesson.

- All things are legitimate matters for prayer:
  the mundane things that worry us; the big things that threaten to overwhelm us; situations and relationships at work that unsettle us and cause anxiety.

- We may not be able to see the connection between prayer and a specific, tangible, and very pressurised situation at work. But the Lord does not only work in ways where we can trace the logic. He works in a way that transcends *all understanding* (v. 7).

Let your mind dwell on the right things (v. 8)

Finally brothers, whatever is true, whatever is noble, whatever is pure, whatever is lovely, whatever is admirable — if anything is excellent or praiseworthy — think about such things. Whatever you have learned or received or heard from me, or seen in me — put it into practice. And the God of peace will be with you.

Philippians 4:8–9

- We need to use our minds, we need to think about the right things, and our minds need to dwell on them.

- Stress can be self-destructive when we obsessively dwell on the wrong things, for example a person who has harmed us.

111

Copy good examples (v. 9)

● Learn from people who are good examples.

● Discuss your problems with people who are sympathetic, experienced, and wiser than you are.

Learn contentment in all circumstances

I rejoice greatly in the Lord that at last you have renewed your concern for me. Indeed, you have been concerned, but you have had no opportunity to show it. I am not saying this because I am in need, for I have learned to be content whatever the circumstances. I know what it is to be in need and I know what it is to have plenty. I have learned the secret of being content in any and every situation, whether living in plenty or in want. I can do everything through him who gives me strength.

Philippians 4: 10–13

● Paul knew that contentment is something independent of circumstances, and does not depend on all the circumstances being ideal.

● Contentment is not something that comes naturally, but has to be learned.

Conclusion

There is no easy answer to dealing with stress in our daily lives. However, Jesus has given us instructions which call for obedience, so that we can enjoy peace through the Holy Spirit. Is it therefore too much to expect that we can enjoy stress-free lives as Christians?

The more Christ is at the centre of what we do, the better we will be able to act without fear of uncertain outcomes but in the secure knowledge of Christ's love and care. That this love and care can be enjoyed wherever we work will be a step of faith for which some will need to have courage.

If we are letting him guide us, no matter what circumstances we face, we will have an inner peace that will be amazing to ourselves and those who know us.

QUESTIONS FOR STUDY

1. Do you think your life is generally more or less pressurised than that of other people you meet and work with?

2. What particular things cause you stress?

3. Read 2 Corinthians 11:24–28. How does Paul's level of stress compare with yours?

4. How well do you think you handle stress?
    On a scale of 1 to 10? Think of a stressful situation you faced this week. Why was it stressful?

5. Do Christians face more or less stress than non-Christians? Why?

6. Share with the group some ways you have found to combat stress.

7. Read Philippians 4:4–11. What biblical principles can you extract that will help you? Read Psalm 127:1–2. What does this add?

8. Do you think God gives us too much to do?

9. Should we consider changing our lifestyle if it subjects us to too much stress?

10. Are there any actions you need to take as a result of having looked at this topic?

FURTHER READING

Specifically On Work Issues

Thank God It's Monday — Ministry In The Workplace
Mark Greene (Scripture Union, 1997)
Well written, fast moving guide to the main issues. Highly recommended.

Issues Facing Christians Today
John Stott (Marshall Morgan & Scott, 1984)
Especially chapter 9, 'Work and Unemployment', and Chapter 10, 'Industrial Relations'. An excellent summary of the theology of work and how it applies practically.

Principles of Conduct
John Murray, (Eerdmans)
See especially chapter 2, 'Creation Ordinances', and chapter 4 'The Ordinance of Labour'.

Work In The Spirit – Towards A Theology Of Work
Miroslav Wolf (OUP, 1991)
Weighty theological exploration.

Business Morality
Peter Vardy (Marshall Morgan & Scott, 1989)
A practical look at the basis for morality in business. Does not base itself specifically on Christianity until the last chapter.

Everything You've Heard Is Wrong
Tony Campolo (Word, 1992)
An excellent explanation of how to put your faith at the centre of your working life, rather than going along with the prevailing world view.

Secular Work Is Full-Time Service
Larry Peabody (CLC, 1988)
If your daily calling is to the secular world, this book reassures you that you are not a second class citizen and shows you how to find joyful fulfilment as you obey God.

Who Switched the Price Tags?
Tony Campolo (Word, 1987)
A search for value in a mixed-up world. Contains a whole section on work, including how to "get a kick" out of work.

The Callings
Paul Helm (Banner of Truth, 1987)

Wake Up to Work
Geoff Shattock (Scripture Union, 1999)
An easy to digest source of advice for workplace friendship and faith.

Champions for God at Work
David Kellett (Terra Nova Publications, 2001)
An encouragement for those in the workplace to be latter-day heroes for God. Practical and offers realistic advice.

Work ... Prison or Place of Destiny?
David Oliver (Word, 1999)
An examination of how the workplace should be viewed as a place where God can shape Christian character and develop spiritual maturity.

Your Work Matters to God
Doug Sherman and William Hendricks (Navpress, 1987)
A clear presentation of a theology of work, and why what we do therefore matters to God because he designed us all uniquely.

Experiencing God
Henry Blackaby and Paul King (Broadman & Holman, 1998)
A thought-provoking introduction to establishing a real relationship with God.

Case Studies

Laing
Roy Coad (Hodder, 1979)
A biography of the Christian civil engineer, John Laing.

Who Profits?
Richard Adams (Lion, 1989)
The fascinating story of the setting up of Traidcraft, Britain's largest independent alternative trading organisation.

Life of George Cadbury
A. G Gardiner (Cassell, 1923)
The amazing story of the Christian behind Cadbury's and the Bourneville experiment. Out of print — try your local library.

A Faith that Works
Don Latham (Terra Nova Publications,1997)
The personal journey of a man committed to seeing God at work in the workplace.

Success

The Search For Significance
Robert S McGee (Word, 1990)
How to get off the performance treadmill and discover why personal success, status, beauty and wealth do not bring lasting happiness.

The Success Factor
Denis Haack (IVP, 1989)
God's view of money, fame, power and self-fulfilment.

Half-Time
Bob Buford (Zondervan, 1994)
A personal guide to moving from success to significance in the middle years of life.

Game Plan
Bob Buford (Zondervan, 1997)
A follow-up to *Half-Time* which helps to identify specific strategies for personal growth.

The Heart of Success
Rob Parsons (Hodder, 2002)
Seven laws for 'Making it in business without losing in life'. Very readable.

Time

Ordering Your Private World
Gordon MacDonald (Highland, 1985)
An excellent guide to sorting out time and priorities before God.

Too Busy Not To Pray
Bill Hybels (Zondervan, 1994)
The busier we are, the more we need to depend on God in
prayer. A gentle reminder.

Money

*Serving God? Serving Mammon? Christians in the Financial
Markets*
Stephen Greene (Marshall Pickering, 1996)

Money, Sex & Power
R. Foster
An excellent analysis of the things that seek to drive and
dominate us.

Tithing
R. T. Kendall (Hodder, 1982)
A concise explanation of the biblical principles behind
tithing.

Money, Possessions and Eternity
Randy Alcorn (Tyndale House)

Your Money and Your Life
Keith Tondeur
A practical guide to what money is about, and how to manage
it.

On-Line Resources

There are an increasing number of online services which provide support to those in the workplace, and which can be delivered direct to desktops via e-mail. These include:

Marketplace Meditations, by Os Hillman at:

www.crosswalk.com
and
www.marketplaceleaders.org

Crosswalk offers a range of devotional resources on different themes, and has a specific focus on supporting and encouraging Christians in the marketplace.

The London Institute of Contemporary Christianity (LICC) also produces a weekly commentary 'Connecting with Culture' which can be delivered direct to e-mail addresses. The address is:

www.licc.org.uk

ABOUT THE AUTHORS

Robin Scurlock lives and worships in Wokingham, Berkshire. He is married to Fay and has two sons, Tom and Matt. He has worked in sales and marketing for eighteen years, with experience in new technologies for the global IT and telecommunications industries. He has travelled in all parts of the world on a variety of consulting assignments, and holds an MBA from Cranfield Business School in the UK. A Christian of some sixteen years, he plays electric violin in his company rock band.

Steve Goss is married to Zoë, is father of Sophie and Emilia, and proud owner of pugs, Ellie and Poppy. He worked in sales and marketing roles for IBM and a television production company, before starting his own marketing and mail order business (whose main claim to fame is running the 'campaign' that saw *Coronation Street*'s Deirdre Rashid released from prison!) He divides his time between his business and leading *Freedom In Christ Ministries*, a UK organisation that equips the church to help Christians take hold of the freedom that Christ won for them.